WALTER THE EDUCATOR'S LITTLE VEGAN RECIPES COOKBOOK

Walter the Educator's Little VEGAN Recipes Cookbook

Walter the Educator

Silent King Books a WhichHead Imprint

Copyright © 2024 by Walter the Educator

All rights reserved. No part of this book may be reproduced in any manner whatsoever without written permission except in the case of brief quotations embodied in critical articles and reviews.

First Printing, 2024

Disclaimer
This book is for entertainment and informational purposes only. The author and publisher offer this information without warranties expressed or implied. No matter the grounds, neither the author nor the publisher will be accountable for any losses, injuries, or other damages caused by the reader's use of this book. The use of this book acknowledges an understanding and acceptance of this disclaimer.

dedicated to all those that enjoy great food

CONTENTS

Dedication v

One - Walter's Vegan Beans Recipe 1

Two - Walter's Vegan Carrot Soup 3

Three - Walter's Vegan Pancakes 5

Four - Walter's Vegan Quinoa And Vegetable Casserole 7

Five - Walter's Vegan Peanut Butter Fudge 10

Six - Walter's Vegan Nut Roast 12

Seven - Walter's Vegan Corn Chowder . . . 14

Eight - Walter's Vegan Chocolate Mousse 16

Nine - Walter's Flavorful Vegan Pasta . . . 18

Ten - Walter's Vegan Granola 20

Eleven - Walter's Vegan Baked Oatmeal Patties 22

Twelve - Walter's Vegan Black Bean Soup . 24

Thirteen - Walter's Vegan Taco Chili 26

Fourteen - Walter's Aromatic Vegan Stew . 28

Fifteen - Walter's Vegan Matcha Crepes . . 30

Sixteen - Walter's Luscious Vegan Chocolate Cake 32

Seventeen - Walter's Vegan Lasagna 35

Eighteen - Walter's Vegan Cookies 38

Nineteen - Walter's Vibrant Vegan Avocado Dip 40

Twenty - Walter's Vegan Curried Rice With Chickpeas And Vegetables 42

Twenty-One - Walter's Vegan Nut And Seed Bread 44

Twenty-Two - Walter's Vegan Lemon Poppy Seed Scones 46

Twenty-Three - Walter's Hearty Vegan Chili 48

Twenty-Four - Walter's Spicy Tantalizing Soup 50

Twenty-Five - Walter's Vegan Spaghetti . . . 53

Twenty-Six - Walter's Banana Blueberry Bliss Muffins 55

Twenty-Seven - Walter's Vegan Potato Medley 57

Twenty-Eight - Walter's Vegan Cornbread . 59

Twenty-Nine - Walter's Vegan Brownies . . . 61

Thirty - Walter's Vegan Fajitas 63

Thirty-One - Walter's Stuffed Tomatoes With Quinoa And Herbs 65

About The Author 67

ONE

WALTER'S VEGAN BEANS RECIPE

Ingredients:
1 cup of dried black beans
1 onion, finely chopped
3 cloves of garlic, minced
1 red bell pepper, diced
1 teaspoon of cumin
1 teaspoon of smoked paprika
1 teaspoon of chili powder
1 can of diced tomatoes
2 cups of vegetable broth
Salt and pepper to taste
Fresh cilantro for garnish
2 tablespoons of olive oil
Instructions:
Rinse the black beans and soak them overnight in

a large bowl of water. Drain and rinse the beans before using.

In a large pot, heat the olive oil over medium heat. Add the chopped onion and sauté until translucent, then add the minced garlic and diced red bell pepper. Cook for a few minutes until the pepper softens.

Stir in the cumin, smoked paprika, and chili powder, and cook for another minute to release the flavors.

Add the soaked black beans to the pot, along with the diced tomatoes and vegetable broth. Bring to a boil, then reduce the heat to a simmer. Cover and cook for 1-1.5 hours, or until the beans are tender.

Once the beans are cooked, season with salt and pepper to taste. If the mixture is too thick, add more vegetable broth as needed.

Serve the vegan beans in bowls, garnished with fresh cilantro. This dish pairs perfectly with steamed rice or crusty bread.

TWO

WALTER'S VEGAN CARROT SOUP

Ingredients:
1 tablespoon of coconut oil
1 onion, finely chopped
3 cloves of garlic, minced
1 tablespoon of fresh ginger, grated
1 teaspoon of ground cumin
1 teaspoon of ground coriander
1/2 teaspoon of turmeric
1/4 teaspoon of cinnamon
1 lb of carrots, peeled and chopped
4 cups of vegetable broth
1 can of coconut milk
Juice of 1 lime
Salt and pepper to taste
Fresh cilantro for garnish

Toasted coconut flakes for garnish

Instructions:

In a large pot, heat the coconut oil over medium heat. Add the chopped onion and sauté until translucent, then add the minced garlic and grated ginger. Cook for a few minutes until fragrant.

Stir in the ground cumin, coriander, turmeric, and cinnamon, and cook for another minute to toast the spices.

Add the chopped carrots to the pot and pour in the vegetable broth. Bring to a boil, then reduce the heat to a simmer. Cover and cook for 20-25 minutes, or until the carrots are tender.

Using an immersion blender, puree the soup until smooth. Alternatively, carefully transfer the soup to a blender and blend in batches until smooth.

Return the pureed soup to the pot and stir in the coconut milk and lime juice. Season with salt and pepper to taste.

Serve the vegan carrot soup in bowls, garnished with fresh cilantro and toasted coconut flakes for an added crunch.

THREE

WALTER'S VEGAN PANCAKES

Ingredients:
1 cup of all-purpose flour
2 tablespoons of sugar
2 teaspoons of baking powder
1/2 teaspoon of baking soda
1/4 teaspoon of salt
1 cup of almond milk (or any non-dairy milk of your choice)
2 tablespoons of apple cider vinegar
2 tablespoons of coconut oil, melted
1 teaspoon of vanilla extract
Fresh berries for topping
Maple syrup for serving
Instructions:
In a medium bowl, whisk together the almond milk

and apple cider vinegar. Let it sit for a few minutes to curdle and create a vegan buttermilk.

In a separate large bowl, whisk together the flour, sugar, baking powder, baking soda, and salt.

Pour the melted coconut oil and vanilla extract into the bowl with the vegan buttermilk and whisk to combine.

Gradually add the wet ingredients to the dry ingredients, stirring until just combined. Be careful not to overmix; a few lumps are okay.

Heat a non-stick pan or griddle over medium heat and lightly grease with coconut oil or cooking spray.

Pour 1/4 cup of batter onto the pan for each pancake. Cook until the edges look set and bubbles form on the surface, then flip and cook until golden brown on the other side.

Repeat with the remaining batter, greasing the pan as needed.

Serve the vegan pancakes topped with fresh berries and a drizzle of maple syrup.

FOUR

WALTER'S VEGAN QUINOA AND VEGETABLE CASSEROLE

Ingredients:
1 cup quinoa, rinsed
2 cups vegetable broth
1 tablespoon olive oil
1 onion, finely chopped
3 garlic cloves, minced
2 carrots, diced
2 bell peppers, diced
1 zucchini, diced
1 cup cherry tomatoes, halved
1 teaspoon dried thyme

1 teaspoon dried oregano
Salt and pepper to taste
1 can (15 oz) chickpeas, drained and rinsed
1/2 cup pitted Kalamata olives, halved
1/4 cup chopped fresh parsley
1/2 cup breadcrumbs
1/4 cup nutritional yeast
2 tablespoons vegan butter, melted
Instructions:

Preheat the oven to 375°F (190°C). Grease a casserole dish with a little olive oil and set aside.

In a medium saucepan, bring the vegetable broth to a boil. Add the quinoa, reduce the heat to low, cover, and simmer for 15-20 minutes, or until the quinoa is cooked and the liquid is absorbed. Fluff with a fork and set aside.

In a large skillet, heat the olive oil over medium heat. Add the chopped onion and garlic, and sauté until fragrant and translucent.

Add the diced carrots, bell peppers, and zucchini to the skillet, and cook until the vegetables are slightly softened.

Stir in the cherry tomatoes, dried thyme, dried oregano, salt, and pepper. Cook for a few more minutes until the tomatoes start to soften.

In a large mixing bowl, combine the cooked quinoa, sautéed vegetables, chickpeas, Kalamata olives, and chopped parsley. Mix until well combined.

Transfer the quinoa and vegetable mixture to the greased casserole dish, spreading it out evenly.

In a small bowl, mix the breadcrumbs, nutritional yeast, and melted vegan butter. Sprinkle the breadcrumb mixture over the top of the casserole.

Cover the casserole dish with foil and bake in the preheated oven for 20 minutes. Then remove the foil and bake for an additional 10-15 minutes, or until the top is golden brown and crispy.

FIVE

WALTER'S VEGAN PEANUT BUTTER FUDGE

Ingredients:
1 cup creamy peanut butter
1/2 cup coconut oil
1/4 cup maple syrup
1 teaspoon vanilla extract
A pinch of salt
Optional: Chopped roasted peanuts for garnish
Instructions:

In a saucepan over low heat, melt the coconut oil and creamy peanut butter together, stirring until smooth and well combined.

Remove the saucepan from the heat and stir in

the maple syrup, vanilla extract, and a pinch of salt, ensuring a homogeneous mixture.

Pour the peanut butter fudge mixture into a parchment paper-lined dish or loaf pan, spreading it evenly.

Optional: Sprinkle the top with chopped roasted peanuts for a delightful crunch and added flavor.

Place the fudge in the refrigerator and allow it to set for at least 2-3 hours, or until firm.

Once set, remove the fudge from the dish and cut it into squares or desired shapes.

Serve and enjoy the delectable vegan peanut butter fudge as a sweet and satisfying treat.

SIX

WALTER'S VEGAN NUT ROAST

Ingredients:
1 cup of mixed nuts (such as almonds, cashews, and walnuts)
1 cup of cooked quinoa
1 cup of finely chopped mushrooms
1 onion, finely diced
2 cloves of garlic, minced
1 tablespoon of balsamic vinegar
2 tablespoons of nutritional yeast
1 tablespoon of soy sauce
1 tablespoon of fresh thyme leaves
1 tablespoon of fresh rosemary, finely chopped
1 tablespoon of ground flaxseeds
1/2 cup of breadcrumbs
Salt and pepper to taste

Olive oil for cooking

Instructions:

Preheat the oven to 350°F (175°C) and lightly grease a loaf pan with olive oil.

In a food processor, pulse the mixed nuts until they are finely chopped but not powdered. Transfer to a large mixing bowl.

In a skillet, heat some olive oil over medium heat and sauté the onions and garlic until translucent. Add the mushrooms and cook until they release their moisture and become golden brown.

Add the cooked quinoa, sautéed mushrooms, onions, balsamic vinegar, nutritional yeast, soy sauce, thyme, rosemary, ground flaxseeds, breadcrumbs, salt, and pepper to the bowl with the chopped nuts. Mix until well combined.

Transfer the mixture into the prepared loaf pan, pressing it down firmly.

Bake for 40-45 minutes or until the top is golden brown and the roast is firm to the touch.

Let it cool for a few minutes before slicing and serving.

SEVEN

WALTER'S VEGAN CORN CHOWDER

Ingredients:
4 cups of fresh corn kernels (about 6 ears of corn)
1 onion, finely chopped
3 cloves of garlic, minced
1 red bell pepper, diced
1 russet potato, peeled and diced
4 cups of vegetable broth
1 can of coconut milk
1 teaspoon of smoked paprika
1 teaspoon of ground cumin
1/2 teaspoon of dried thyme
1/4 teaspoon of cayenne pepper
Juice of 1 lime
Salt and pepper to taste
Chopped fresh cilantro for garnish

Olive oil for cooking

Instructions:

In a large pot, heat some olive oil over medium heat. Add the chopped onion and sauté until translucent, then add the minced garlic and cook for another minute.

Add the diced red bell pepper and potato to the pot, and cook for a few minutes until the vegetables start to soften.

Stir in the fresh corn kernels and cook for a couple of minutes, allowing the flavors to meld.

Pour in the vegetable broth and coconut milk, and then add the smoked paprika, ground cumin, dried thyme, and cayenne pepper. Bring the chowder to a gentle simmer and let it cook for about 15-20 minutes, or until the potatoes are tender.

Using an immersion blender, blend a portion of the chowder to thicken the base while still leaving some chunky texture.

Stir in the lime juice and season with salt and pepper to taste.

Ladle the vegan corn chowder into bowls and garnish with chopped fresh cilantro.

EIGHT

WALTER'S VEGAN CHOCOLATE MOUSSE

Ingredients:
1 can of full-fat coconut milk, chilled overnight
1 cup of vegan dark chocolate, chopped
2 tablespoons of maple syrup
1 teaspoon of pure vanilla extract
Fresh berries for garnish
Vegan whipped cream for garnish (optional)
Instructions:
Chill a mixing bowl in the refrigerator for at least 15 minutes before starting the recipe.
Open the chilled can of coconut milk and scoop out the solid coconut cream that has risen to the top, leaving the liquid behind. Place the coconut cream into the chilled mixing bowl.
Using a hand mixer or stand mixer, whip the coconut

cream until it becomes light and fluffy.

In a heatproof bowl, melt the vegan dark chocolate over a double boiler or in the microwave in 30-second intervals, stirring until smooth.

Once the chocolate is melted, let it cool slightly before gently folding it into the whipped coconut cream.

Add the maple syrup and pure vanilla extract to the mixture, and continue to gently fold until everything is well combined.

Transfer the vegan chocolate mousse into serving glasses or ramekins, and refrigerate for at least 2 hours, or until set.

Before serving, garnish with fresh berries and a dollop of vegan whipped cream if desired.

NINE

WALTER'S FLAVORFUL VEGAN PASTA

Ingredients:
1 cup of brown lentils
8 ounces of whole wheat pasta
2 tablespoons of olive oil
1 large red onion, sliced
3 cloves of garlic, minced
4 cups of chopped kale
1 cup of vegetable broth
1 teaspoon of smoked paprika
1/2 teaspoon of cumin
1/4 teaspoon of red pepper flakes
Salt and pepper to taste
2 tablespoons of nutritional yeast
Fresh parsley for garnish
Instructions:

Cook the lentils according to package instructions until tender, then drain and set aside.

Cook the pasta in a large pot of boiling salted water until al dente, then drain and set aside.

In a large skillet, heat the olive oil over medium heat.

Add the sliced red onion and cook until caramelized, about 10 minutes.

Add the minced garlic to the skillet and cook for an additional 2 minutes.

Stir in the chopped kale and cook until wilted, about 5 minutes.

Pour in the vegetable broth, smoked paprika, cumin, and red pepper flakes. Season with salt and pepper to taste.

Add the cooked lentils to the skillet and stir to combine all the ingredients.

Toss in the cooked pasta and stir until everything is well mixed and heated through.

Sprinkle nutritional yeast over the pasta and toss to coat.

Serve the Lentil, Kale, and Red Onion Pasta in individual bowls, garnished with fresh parsley.

TEN

WALTER'S VEGAN GRANOLA

Ingredients:
2 cups rolled oats
1/2 cup raw almonds, chopped
1/2 cup raw cashews, chopped
1/2 cup unsweetened shredded coconut
1/4 cup pumpkin seeds
1/4 cup sunflower seeds
1/4 cup coconut oil, melted
1/3 cup maple syrup
1 teaspoon vanilla extract
1/2 teaspoon ground cinnamon
1/4 teaspoon sea salt
1/2 cup dried cranberries
1/2 cup dried apricots, chopped
Instructions:

Preheat the oven to 325°F (160°C) and line a baking sheet with parchment paper.

In a large bowl, combine the rolled oats, chopped almonds, chopped cashews, shredded coconut, pumpkin seeds, and sunflower seeds.

In a separate small bowl, whisk together the melted coconut oil, maple syrup, vanilla extract, ground cinnamon, and sea salt.

Pour the wet mixture over the dry ingredients and stir until everything is well coated.

Spread the mixture evenly onto the prepared baking sheet.

Bake for 20-25 minutes, stirring halfway through, until the granola is golden brown and fragrant.

Remove from the oven and let the granola cool completely on the baking sheet.

Once cooled, stir in the dried cranberries and chopped apricots.

Transfer the vegan granola to an airtight container for storage.

ELEVEN

WALTER'S VEGAN BAKED OATMEAL PATTIES

Ingredients:
2 cups rolled oats
1 ripe banana, mashed
1/4 cup almond butter
1/4 cup maple syrup
1/4 cup unsweetened almond milk
1 teaspoon vanilla extract
1/2 teaspoon ground cinnamon
1/4 teaspoon ground nutmeg
1/4 teaspoon sea salt
1/2 cup dried blueberries
1/4 cup chopped walnuts

1/4 cup shredded coconut

Instructions:

Preheat the oven to 350°F (175°C) and line a baking sheet with parchment paper.

In a large bowl, combine the rolled oats, mashed banana, almond butter, maple syrup, almond milk, vanilla extract, ground cinnamon, ground nutmeg, and sea salt. Mix until well combined.

Fold in the dried blueberries, chopped walnuts, and shredded coconut, ensuring they are evenly distributed throughout the mixture.

Using a spoon or cookie scoop, form the oatmeal mixture into patties and place them on the prepared baking sheet.

Bake for 20-25 minutes, or until the oatmeal patties are golden and set.

Remove from the oven and let the patties cool on the baking sheet for a few minutes before transferring them to a wire rack to cool completely.

TWELVE

WALTER'S VEGAN BLACK BEAN SOUP

Ingredients:
2 tablespoons olive oil
1 large red onion, finely chopped
3 cloves garlic, minced
2 carrots, diced
2 stalks celery, diced
1 red bell pepper, diced
1 teaspoon ground cumin
1 teaspoon smoked paprika
1/2 teaspoon chili powder
1/4 teaspoon cayenne pepper
4 cups vegetable broth
3 (15 oz) cans black beans, drained and rinsed
1 (14 oz) can diced tomatoes
1 cup corn kernels

2 tablespoons tomato paste
Juice of 1 lime
Salt and pepper to taste
Fresh cilantro for garnish
Instructions:

In a large pot, heat the olive oil over medium heat. Add the chopped red onion and cook until softened, about 5 minutes.

Add the minced garlic, diced carrots, diced celery, and diced red bell pepper to the pot. Cook for another 5 minutes, stirring occasionally.

Stir in the ground cumin, smoked paprika, chili powder, and cayenne pepper, and cook for 1-2 minutes to toast the spices.

Pour in the vegetable broth, black beans, diced tomatoes, and corn kernels. Stir in the tomato paste and bring the soup to a simmer.

Let the soup simmer for 20-25 minutes, stirring occasionally, until the vegetables are tender and the flavors have melded together.

Use an immersion blender to partially blend the soup, leaving some beans and vegetables whole for texture.

Squeeze in the lime juice and season the soup with salt and pepper to taste.

Serve the vegan black bean soup in individual bowls, garnished with fresh cilantro.

THIRTEEN

WALTER'S VEGAN TACO CHILI

Ingredients:
1 tablespoon olive oil
1 red onion, diced
3 garlic cloves, minced
1 red bell pepper, diced
1 yellow bell pepper, diced
1 jalapeño, seeded and diced
1 tablespoon chili powder
1 teaspoon ground cumin
1 teaspoon smoked paprika
1 teaspoon dried oregano
1 can (15 oz) black beans, drained and rinsed
1 can (15 oz) kidney beans, drained and rinsed
1 can (15 oz) corn kernels, drained
1 can (15 oz) diced tomatoes

1 cup vegetable broth
1 tablespoon tomato paste
Juice of 1 lime
Salt and pepper to taste
Fresh cilantro for garnish
Instructions:

In a large pot, heat the olive oil over medium heat. Add the diced red onion, minced garlic, diced red and yellow bell peppers, and diced jalapeño. Cook until the vegetables are softened, about 5-7 minutes.

Stir in the chili powder, ground cumin, smoked paprika, and dried oregano, and cook for another 2 minutes to toast the spices.

Add the black beans, kidney beans, corn kernels, diced tomatoes, vegetable broth, and tomato paste to the pot. Stir to combine all the ingredients.

Bring the chili to a simmer and let it cook for 20-25 minutes, stirring occasionally.

Squeeze in the lime juice and season the chili with salt and pepper to taste.

Serve the vegan taco chili in individual bowls, garnished with fresh cilantro.

FOURTEEN

WALTER'S AROMATIC VEGAN STEW

Ingredients:
2 tablespoons olive oil
1 large onion, finely chopped
3 garlic cloves, minced
1 teaspoon ground cumin
1 teaspoon ground coriander
1/2 teaspoon ground turmeric
1/2 teaspoon ground cinnamon
1/4 teaspoon cayenne pepper
1 can (14 oz) diced tomatoes
1 can (14 oz) chickpeas, drained and rinsed
3 cups vegetable broth
1 cup diced carrots
1 cup diced sweet potatoes
1 cup diced zucchini

1/4 cup chopped dried apricots
2 tablespoons tomato paste
Salt and pepper to taste
Fresh cilantro for garnish
Cooked couscous or quinoa for serving
Instructions:

In a large pot, heat the olive oil over medium heat. Add the chopped onion and sauté until softened, about 5 minutes. Add the minced garlic and cook for an additional 2 minutes.

Stir in the ground cumin, coriander, turmeric, cinnamon, and cayenne pepper. Cook for 1-2 minutes to toast the spices and release their flavors.

Add the diced tomatoes, chickpeas, and vegetable broth to the pot. Stir in the diced carrots, sweet potatoes, and zucchini.

Bring the stew to a simmer and let it cook for 20-25 minutes, or until the vegetables are tender.

Stir in the chopped dried apricots and tomato paste. Season the stew with salt and pepper to taste.

Serve the Vegan Moroccan Chickpea Stew in individual bowls, garnished with fresh cilantro. Serve with cooked couscous or quinoa for a complete and satisfying meal.

FIFTEEN

WALTER'S VEGAN MATCHA CREPES

Ingredients:
1 cup all-purpose flour
1 1/2 cups almond milk (or any plant-based milk of choice)
1 tablespoon maple syrup
1 tablespoon coconut oil, melted
1 teaspoon matcha powder
1/2 teaspoon vanilla extract
Pinch of salt
Coconut oil for greasing the pan
Instructions:
In a mixing bowl, whisk together the all-purpose flour, almond milk, maple syrup, melted coconut oil, matcha powder, vanilla extract, and a pinch of salt until the batter is smooth and well combined.

Let the batter rest for about 10-15 minutes to allow the flavors to meld together.

Heat a non-stick skillet or crepe pan over medium heat and lightly grease it with coconut oil.

Pour a ladleful of the batter into the center of the pan, then quickly tilt and swirl the pan to spread the batter evenly into a thin, round crepe.

Cook the crepe for about 1-2 minutes, or until the edges start to lift and the bottom is lightly golden.

Carefully flip the crepe using a spatula and cook for an additional 1-2 minutes on the other side.

Transfer the cooked crepe to a plate and repeat the process with the remaining batter, greasing the pan as needed.

Once all the crepes are cooked, serve them with your favorite vegan toppings such as fresh berries, dairy-free yogurt, or a drizzle of maple syrup.

SIXTEEN

WALTER'S LUSCIOUS VEGAN CHOCOLATE CAKE

Ingredients:
2 cups all-purpose flour
1 1/2 cups granulated sugar
1/2 cup unsweetened cocoa powder
1 1/2 tsp baking powder
1 1/2 tsp baking soda
1/2 tsp salt
1 1/2 cups almond milk
1/2 cup coconut oil, melted
2 tsp pure vanilla extract
1 cup strong brewed coffee, cooled
1/2 cup dairy-free dark chocolate chips

1 tbsp apple cider vinegar

Instructions:

Preheat the oven to 350°F (175°C). Grease and flour two 9-inch round cake pans.

In a large bowl, sift together the flour, sugar, cocoa powder, baking powder, baking soda, and salt.

In a separate bowl, whisk together the almond milk, melted coconut oil, and vanilla extract.

Add the wet ingredients to the dry ingredients and mix until well combined.

Stir in the brewed coffee until the batter is smooth.

Fold in the dark chocolate chips.

Quickly stir in the apple cider vinegar, then pour the batter into the prepared cake pans.

Bake for 30-35 minutes, or until a toothpick inserted into the center of the cakes comes out clean.

Allow the cakes to cool in the pans for 10 minutes before transferring them to a wire rack to cool completely.

Chocolate Ganache Frosting:

Ingredients:

1 1/2 cups dairy-free dark chocolate, chopped

1 cup coconut cream

2 tbsp maple syrup

1 tsp vanilla extract

Instructions:

In a heatproof bowl, combine the chopped dark chocolate, coconut cream, and maple syrup.

Place the bowl over a pot of simmering water, stirring

until the chocolate is melted and the mixture is smooth.

Remove from heat and stir in the vanilla extract.

Allow the ganache to cool and thicken slightly before frosting the cake.

Once the cakes have cooled, spread a generous layer of the chocolate ganache frosting between the two layers and over the top and sides of the cake. Garnish with fresh berries, edible flowers, or shredded coconut for an extra touch of elegance. Enjoy this luscious vegan chocolate cake with friends and family!

SEVENTEEN

WALTER'S VEGAN LASAGNA

Ingredients:
1 box lasagna noodles (look for egg-free varieties)
1 large eggplant, sliced into thin rounds
1 large zucchini, sliced into thin rounds
1 large yellow squash, sliced into thin rounds
1 cup sliced mushrooms
1 onion, diced
3 cloves garlic, minced
1 can (28 oz) crushed tomatoes
1 can (15 oz) tomato sauce
2 tbsp tomato paste
1 tbsp balsamic vinegar
1 tsp dried oregano
1 tsp dried basil
1/2 tsp red pepper flakes

Salt and pepper to taste
2 cups baby spinach
2 cups raw cashews, soaked and drained
1 1/2 cups unsweetened almond milk
2 tbsp nutritional yeast
1 tbsp lemon juice
1/2 tsp garlic powder
1/4 tsp onion powder
Fresh basil leaves for garnish
Instructions:

Preheat the oven to 375°F (190°C). Grease a 9x13 inch baking dish.

Cook the lasagna noodles according to the package instructions. Drain and set aside.

In a large skillet, sauté the diced onion and minced garlic until fragrant. Add the sliced mushrooms and cook until they release their moisture.

Pour in the crushed tomatoes, tomato sauce, tomato paste, balsamic vinegar, oregano, basil, red pepper flakes, salt, and pepper. Let the sauce simmer for 10-15 minutes.

In a separate pan, grill the eggplant, zucchini, and yellow squash until lightly browned on both sides. Set aside.

In a blender, combine the soaked cashews, almond milk, nutritional yeast, lemon juice, garlic powder, and onion powder. Blend until smooth and creamy.

To assemble the lasagna, spread a thin layer of the tomato sauce on the bottom of the prepared baking dish. Arrange a layer of lasagna noodles on top, followed by a layer of grilled vegetables, a handful of baby spinach, and a generous drizzle of the cashew cream sauce. Repeat the layers until all ingredients are used, finishing with a final layer of cashew cream sauce on top.

Cover the baking dish with foil and bake for 30 minutes. Remove the foil and bake for an additional 10-15 minutes, or until the top is golden and bubbly.

Let the lasagna rest for 10-15 minutes before slicing. Garnish with fresh basil leaves before serving.

EIGHTEEN

WALTER'S VEGAN COOKIES

Ingredients:
2 1/4 cups whole wheat flour
1 tsp baking soda
1/2 tsp salt
1 cup coconut sugar
1/2 cup coconut oil, melted
1/4 cup unsweetened applesauce
1 tsp pure vanilla extract
1/2 cup dairy-free chocolate chips
1/4 cup chopped walnuts or almonds (optional)
Instructions:
Preheat the oven to 350°F (175°C). Line a baking sheet with parchment paper.
In a medium bowl, whisk together the whole wheat flour, baking soda, and salt.

In a separate bowl, cream together the coconut sugar and melted coconut oil until well combined.

Add the applesauce and vanilla extract to the sugar mixture and mix until smooth.

Gradually add the dry ingredients to the wet ingredients, mixing until a dough forms.

Fold in the dairy-free chocolate chips and chopped nuts, if using.

Using a cookie scoop or spoon, portion the dough onto the prepared baking sheet, leaving space between each cookie.

Gently flatten each cookie with the back of a spoon or fork.

Bake for 10-12 minutes, or until the edges are golden brown.

Allow the cookies to cool on the baking sheet for a few minutes before transferring them to a wire rack to cool completely.

NINETEEN

WALTER'S VIBRANT VEGAN AVOCADO DIP

Ingredients:
2 ripe avocados
1/4 cup diced red onion
1/4 cup diced tomato
1/4 cup chopped fresh cilantro
2 tbsp lime juice
1 clove garlic, minced
1/2 tsp cumin
1/2 tsp chili powder
Salt and pepper to taste
Instructions:

Cut the avocados in half, remove the pits, and scoop the flesh into a mixing bowl.

Mash the avocados with a fork until creamy, leaving some small chunks for texture.

Add the diced red onion, diced tomato, chopped cilantro, lime juice, minced garlic, cumin, chili powder, salt, and pepper to the mashed avocado. Mix well to combine all the ingredients.

Taste the avocado dip and adjust the seasoning, if needed, to suit your preferences.

Transfer the dip to a serving bowl and garnish with additional chopped cilantro and a sprinkle of chili powder.

Serve the avocado dip with your favorite tortilla chips, fresh vegetable sticks, or as a flavorful topping for tacos and burritos.

TWENTY

WALTER'S VEGAN CURRIED RICE WITH CHICKPEAS AND VEGETABLES

Ingredients:
1 cup basmati rice
1 3/4 cups vegetable broth
1 tbsp coconut oil
1 small onion, finely chopped
2 cloves garlic, minced
1 tbsp curry powder
1/2 tsp ground turmeric
1/2 tsp ground cumin
1/2 tsp ground coriander
1/4 tsp cayenne pepper (optional for heat)

1 cup diced carrots
1 cup diced bell peppers
1 cup cooked chickpeas
1/4 cup raisins
1/4 cup chopped fresh cilantro
Salt and pepper to taste
Instructions:

Rinse the basmati rice under cold water until the water runs clear. Drain the rice and set aside.

In a medium saucepan, heat the coconut oil over medium heat. Add the chopped onion and garlic, and sauté until softened and fragrant.

Stir in the curry powder, turmeric, cumin, coriander, and cayenne pepper, and cook for another minute to toast the spices.

Add the diced carrots and bell peppers to the pan, and sauté for a few minutes until they begin to soften.

Add the basmati rice to the pan and stir to coat the rice with the aromatic vegetables and spices.

Pour in the vegetable broth and bring the mixture to a gentle boil. Reduce the heat to low, cover the saucepan, and let the rice simmer for 15-20 minutes, or until the liquid is absorbed and the rice is tender.

Once the rice is cooked, fluff it with a fork and gently fold in the cooked chickpeas and raisins. Season with salt and pepper to taste.

Sprinkle the curried rice with fresh cilantro before serving.

TWENTY-ONE

WALTER'S VEGAN NUT AND SEED BREAD

Ingredients:
3 cups all-purpose flour
1 cup whole wheat flour
1 packet (2 1/4 tsp) active dry yeast
1 1/2 cups warm water
1/4 cup maple syrup
1/4 cup olive oil
1 tsp salt
1/2 cup chopped mixed nuts and seeds (such as walnuts, pumpkin seeds, and sunflower seeds)
2 tbsp rolled oats for topping
Instructions:

In a large mixing bowl, combine the warm water and maple syrup. Sprinkle the yeast over the mixture and let it sit for 5-10 minutes, or until the yeast becomes frothy.

Stir in the olive oil and salt until well combined.

Gradually add the all-purpose flour and whole wheat flour, mixing until a dough forms.

Turn the dough out onto a floured surface and knead for 8-10 minutes, or until the dough becomes smooth and elastic.

Place the dough in a greased bowl, cover with a clean kitchen towel, and let it rise in a warm place for 1-1.5 hours, or until doubled in size.

Preheat the oven to 375°F (190°C). Lightly grease a 9x5-inch loaf pan.

Punch down the risen dough and knead in the chopped nuts and seeds until evenly distributed.

Shape the dough into a loaf and place it in the prepared loaf pan. Sprinkle the top with rolled oats.

Cover the pan with the kitchen towel and let the dough rise for an additional 30-45 minutes.

Bake the bread in the preheated oven for 35-40 minutes, or until the top is golden brown and the loaf sounds hollow when tapped on the bottom.

Remove the bread from the pan and let it cool on a wire rack before slicing.

TWENTY-TWO

WALTER'S VEGAN LEMON POPPY SEED SCONES

Ingredients:
2 cups all-purpose flour
1/4 cup granulated sugar
1 tablespoon baking powder
1/4 teaspoon salt
Zest of 2 lemons
1/2 cup cold coconut oil
1/2 cup non-dairy milk
1 tablespoon lemon juice
2 tablespoons poppy seeds
For the glaze:
1 cup powdered sugar

2-3 tablespoons fresh lemon juice

Instructions:

Preheat the oven to 400°F (200°C) and line a baking sheet with parchment paper.

In a large mixing bowl, whisk together the flour, sugar, baking powder, salt, and lemon zest.

Cut the cold coconut oil into the flour mixture using a pastry cutter or fork until it resembles coarse crumbs.

In a separate bowl, mix the non-dairy milk and lemon juice. Pour the wet mixture into the dry ingredients and stir until just combined.

Gently fold in the poppy seeds until evenly distributed.

Transfer the dough to a floured surface and pat it into a circle about 1 inch thick. Cut the circle into 8 wedges and place them on the prepared baking sheet.

Bake for 15-18 minutes, or until the scones are golden brown.

While the scones are cooling, prepare the glaze by whisking together the powdered sugar and enough lemon juice to achieve a thick but pourable consistency.

Drizzle the glaze over the cooled scones and let it set before serving.

TWENTY-THREE

WALTER'S HEARTY VEGAN CHILI

Ingredients:
1 tablespoon olive oil
1 large onion, diced
3 cloves garlic, minced
1 red bell pepper, diced
1 green bell pepper, diced
2 medium carrots, diced
1 zucchini, diced
1 cup corn kernels
1 can (15 oz) black beans, drained and rinsed
1 can (15 oz) kidney beans, drained and rinsed
1 can (15 oz) diced tomatoes
1 can (15 oz) tomato sauce
2 cups vegetable broth
2 tablespoons chili powder

1 teaspoon cumin
1 teaspoon smoked paprika
1 teaspoon oregano
Salt and pepper to taste
Fresh cilantro, for garnish
Avocado slices, for garnish
Lime wedges, for serving
Instructions:

In a large pot, heat the olive oil over medium heat. Add the diced onion and garlic, and sauté until the onion is translucent and fragrant.

Add the diced bell peppers, carrots, and zucchini to the pot. Cook for 5-7 minutes, or until the vegetables begin to soften.

Stir in the corn, black beans, kidney beans, diced tomatoes, tomato sauce, and vegetable broth.

Add the chili powder, cumin, smoked paprika, oregano, salt, and pepper to the pot. Stir well to combine all the ingredients.

Bring the chili to a simmer, then reduce the heat to low and let it cook for 30-40 minutes, stirring occasionally, to allow the flavors to meld together.

Adjust the seasoning to taste, adding more salt and pepper if necessary.

Serve the vegan chili hot, garnished with fresh cilantro and avocado slices. Squeeze a wedge of lime over each serving for an extra burst of citrusy flavor.

TWENTY-FOUR

WALTER'S SPICY TANTALIZING SOUP

Ingredients:
1 tablespoon of coconut oil
1 large red onion, finely chopped
3 cloves of garlic, minced
2 large carrots, diced
2 celery stalks, chopped
1 red bell pepper, diced
1 yellow bell pepper, diced
1 teaspoon of ground cumin
1 teaspoon of smoked paprika
1/2 teaspoon of cayenne pepper
1 teaspoon of turmeric
1 can of diced tomatoes
4 cups of vegetable broth
1 cup of red lentils

1 can of black beans, drained and rinsed
Salt and black pepper to taste
Fresh cilantro for garnish
Sliced avocado for garnish
Lime wedges for serving
Instructions:

In a large pot, heat the coconut oil over medium heat. Add the chopped red onion and minced garlic and sauté until fragrant and translucent.

Add the diced carrots, chopped celery, and diced bell peppers to the pot, and cook for a few minutes until the vegetables begin to soften.

Sprinkle in the ground cumin, smoked paprika, cayenne pepper, and turmeric, stirring to coat the vegetables with the aromatic spices.

Pour in the can of diced tomatoes and vegetable broth, then add the red lentils and black beans. Stir the soup well and bring it to a gentle boil.

Reduce the heat to a simmer and let the soup cook for about 20-25 minutes, or until the lentils are tender and the flavors have melded together.

Season the soup with salt and black pepper to taste, adjusting the level of spiciness to your preference.

Ladle the Fiery Vegan Pepper Pot Soup into bowls and garnish with fresh cilantro, sliced avocado, and a squeeze of lime juice.

Serve the soup alongside crusty bread or a side of quinoa for a hearty and satisfying meal.

This tantalizing soup is a celebration of vibrant flavors

and nourishing ingredients, making it the perfect dish to warm your body and invigorate your senses. Enjoy the robust and spicy flavors of this Fiery Vegan Pepper Pot Soup as it transports you to a world of culinary delight.

TWENTY-FIVE

WALTER'S VEGAN SPAGHETTI

Ingredients:
8 oz whole wheat spaghetti
1 tbsp olive oil
1 yellow onion, finely diced
3 cloves of garlic, minced
1 red bell pepper, thinly sliced
1 cup sliced mushrooms
1 can (14 oz) diced tomatoes
2 tbsp tomato paste
1 tsp dried oregano
1 tsp dried basil
1/2 tsp red pepper flakes
Salt and pepper to taste
Fresh basil leaves for garnish

Vegan parmesan cheese (optional)

Instructions:

Cook the spaghetti according to the package instructions until al dente. Drain and set aside.

In a large skillet, heat the olive oil over medium heat. Add the diced onion and sauté until translucent, then add the minced garlic and cook for another minute.

Add the sliced red bell pepper and mushrooms to the skillet, and cook until the vegetables are tender.

Stir in the diced tomatoes, tomato paste, dried oregano, dried basil, red pepper flakes, and season with salt and pepper. Let the sauce simmer for 10-15 minutes to allow the flavors to meld together.

Add the cooked spaghetti to the skillet and toss to coat the pasta with the sauce.

Serve the vegan spaghetti in individual bowls, garnished with fresh basil leaves and a sprinkle of vegan parmesan cheese, if desired.

TWENTY-SIX

WALTER'S BANANA BLUEBERRY BLISS MUFFINS

Ingredients:
1 1/2 cups of all-purpose flour
1 teaspoon of baking powder
1/2 teaspoon of baking soda
1/4 teaspoon of salt
1/2 teaspoon of ground cinnamon
2 ripe bananas, mashed
1/2 cup of brown sugar
1/4 cup of coconut oil, melted
1 flax egg (1 tablespoon ground flaxseed + 3 tablespoons water, mixed and set aside for 5 minutes)
1 teaspoon of vanilla extract
1 cup of fresh blueberries

Zest of 1 lemon
1/4 cup of chopped walnuts (optional)
Instructions:

Preheat the oven to 375°F (190°C) and line a muffin tin with paper liners or lightly grease the tin.

In a large bowl, whisk together the flour, baking powder, baking soda, salt, and ground cinnamon.

In another bowl, combine the mashed bananas, brown sugar, melted coconut oil, flax egg, and vanilla extract. Mix until well combined.

Gently fold the wet ingredients into the dry ingredients until just combined. Be careful not to overmix.

Carefully fold in the fresh blueberries, lemon zest, and chopped walnuts (if using) into the batter.

Spoon the batter into the prepared muffin tin, filling each cup about three-quarters full.

Bake the muffins for 20-25 minutes, or until a toothpick inserted into the center comes out clean.

Allow the muffins to cool in the tin for 5 minutes before transferring them to a wire rack to cool completely.

TWENTY-SEVEN

WALTER'S VEGAN POTATO MEDLEY

Ingredients:

2 lbs of mixed baby potatoes (red, yellow, and purple), halved

3 tablespoons of olive oil

4 garlic cloves, minced

1 tablespoon of chopped fresh rosemary

1 tablespoon of chopped fresh thyme

1 tablespoon of chopped fresh parsley

1 teaspoon of smoked paprika

Salt and pepper to taste

Zest of 1 lemon

2 tablespoons of nutritional yeast (optional for a cheesy flavor)

Instructions:

Preheat the oven to 400°F (200°C) and line a baking

sheet with parchment paper.

In a large bowl, toss the halved baby potatoes with olive oil, minced garlic, chopped rosemary, thyme, parsley, smoked paprika, salt, and pepper until evenly coated.

Spread the seasoned potatoes in a single layer on the prepared baking sheet.

Roast the potatoes in the preheated oven for 30-35 minutes, or until they are golden and crispy on the outside, and tender on the inside.

Once the potatoes are cooked, remove them from the oven and sprinkle with lemon zest and nutritional yeast, if using.

Transfer the herb-roasted vegan potato medley to a serving dish and garnish with additional fresh herbs if desired.

This savory herb-roasted vegan potato medley is a delightful blend of earthy flavors and aromatic herbs, with a crispy exterior and a fluffy interior. The combination of mixed baby potatoes, fragrant herbs, and a hint of citrus zest creates a mouthwatering dish that is sure to impress even the most discerning palate. Enjoy this delectable potato medley as a side dish or a satisfying main course!

TWENTY-EIGHT

WALTER'S VEGAN CORNBREAD

Ingredients:
1 cup of cornmeal
1 cup of all-purpose flour
1 tablespoon of baking powder
1/2 teaspoon of baking soda
1/2 teaspoon of salt
1 cup of unsweetened almond milk
1/4 cup of maple syrup
1/4 cup of melted coconut oil
1 tablespoon of apple cider vinegar
1 cup of corn kernels (fresh, canned, or frozen)
1 jalapeño, seeded and finely chopped
1/4 cup of chopped green onions
1/4 cup of chopped fresh cilantro
Instructions:

Preheat the oven to 375°F (190°C) and lightly grease a square baking dish.

In a large bowl, whisk together the cornmeal, all-purpose flour, baking powder, baking soda, and salt.

In a separate bowl, combine the almond milk, maple syrup, melted coconut oil, and apple cider vinegar. Mix well.

Pour the wet ingredients into the dry ingredients and stir until just combined. Be careful not to overmix.

Gently fold in the corn kernels, chopped jalapeño, green onions, and cilantro until evenly distributed in the batter.

Pour the batter into the prepared baking dish and smooth the top.

Bake the cornbread for 25-30 minutes, or until the top is golden brown and a toothpick inserted into the center comes out clean.

Allow the cornbread to cool in the pan for 10 minutes before slicing and serving.

This delectable vegan cornbread is a harmonious blend of sweet, savory, and slightly spicy flavors, with the delightful crunch of fresh corn kernels and a hint of heat from the jalapeño. The addition of green onions and cilantro adds a burst of freshness, making this cornbread a perfect accompaniment to soups, stews, or enjoyed on its own as a delightful snack. Enjoy the mouthwatering goodness of this unique vegan cornbread recipe!

TWENTY-NINE

WALTER'S VEGAN BROWNIES

Ingredients:
1 cup all-purpose flour
1/2 cup unsweetened cocoa powder
1 teaspoon baking powder
1/2 teaspoon salt
1/2 cup coconut oil, melted
1 cup coconut sugar
1/4 cup unsweetened applesauce
1 teaspoon vanilla extract
1/2 cup dairy-free chocolate chips
1/2 cup chopped walnuts (optional)

Instructions:

Preheat the oven to 350°F (175°C) and lightly grease an 8x8 inch baking dish.

In a large bowl, whisk together the flour, cocoa powder,

baking powder, and salt until well combined.

In a separate bowl, mix the melted coconut oil, coconut sugar, applesauce, and vanilla extract until smooth.

Gradually add the wet ingredients to the dry ingredients and mix until a thick, smooth batter forms.

Fold in the dairy-free chocolate chips and chopped walnuts, if using.

Pour the batter into the prepared baking dish and spread it evenly.

Bake for 25-30 minutes, or until the edges are set and a toothpick inserted into the center comes out with a few moist crumbs.

Allow the brownies to cool in the pan for at least 15 minutes before slicing into squares.

These delectable vegan brownies are a delightful indulgence, with a rich, fudgy texture and a deep chocolate flavor. The addition of dairy-free chocolate chips and walnuts provides a satisfying crunch and extra decadence to each bite. Enjoy these mouthwatering vegan brownies as a sweet treat for any occasion!

THIRTY

WALTER'S VEGAN FAJITAS

Ingredients:
1 tablespoon olive oil
1 red onion, sliced
1 red bell pepper, sliced
1 yellow bell pepper, sliced
1 green bell pepper, sliced
1 cup sliced mushrooms
1 teaspoon ground cumin
1 teaspoon smoked paprika
1 teaspoon chili powder
1 teaspoon garlic powder
1 teaspoon onion powder
Juice of 1 lime
Salt and pepper to taste
8 small flour tortillas

Fresh cilantro, chopped, for garnish
Avocado slices, for serving
Vegan sour cream, for serving
Salsa, for serving

Instructions:

Heat the olive oil in a large skillet over medium-high heat.

Add the sliced red onion, red bell pepper, yellow bell pepper, green bell pepper, and mushrooms to the skillet. Sauté for 5-7 minutes, or until the vegetables are tender-crisp.

Sprinkle the ground cumin, smoked paprika, chili powder, garlic powder, and onion powder over the vegetables. Stir to combine and cook for an additional 2 minutes.

Squeeze the lime juice over the fajita mixture and season with salt and pepper to taste. Stir well.

Warm the flour tortillas in a separate skillet or in the microwave.

To assemble the fajitas, spoon the vegetable mixture onto the warm tortillas. Top with fresh cilantro, avocado slices, and a dollop of vegan sour cream. Serve with salsa on the side.

These mouthwatering vegan fajitas are bursting with vibrant flavors and textures, making them a delightful addition to any plant-based meal repertoire. Enjoy!

THIRTY-ONE

WALTER'S STUFFED TOMATOES WITH QUINOA AND HERBS

Ingredients:
4 large beefsteak tomatoes
1 cup quinoa, cooked
1 small red onion, finely chopped
2 cloves garlic, minced
1 cup baby spinach, chopped
1/4 cup fresh basil, chopped
1/4 cup fresh parsley, chopped
1/4 cup pine nuts, toasted
1/4 cup panko breadcrumbs
2 tablespoons nutritional yeast
2 tablespoons olive oil
Salt and pepper to taste

Fresh basil leaves, for garnish
Balsamic glaze, for drizzling
Instructions:
   Preheat the oven to 375°F (190°C).
Cut the tops off the tomatoes and scoop out the seeds and flesh, leaving a sturdy shell. Reserve the tomato flesh for later use.
In a large bowl, combine the cooked quinoa, red onion, garlic, baby spinach, chopped basil, chopped parsley, toasted pine nuts, panko breadcrumbs, nutritional yeast, and olive oil. Mix well and season with salt and pepper.
Stuff each hollowed-out tomato with the quinoa mixture, pressing it down gently.
Place the stuffed tomatoes on a baking sheet and bake for 25-30 minutes, or until the tomatoes are tender and the filling is golden brown.
Remove the stuffed tomatoes from the oven and let them cool slightly.
Garnish with fresh basil leaves and a drizzle of balsamic glaze before serving.
These savory stuffed tomatoes with quinoa and herbs are a delightful fusion of flavors and textures, making them a delectable addition to any vegan culinary repertoire. Enjoy!

ABOUT THE AUTHOR

Walter the Educator is one of the pseudonyms for Walter Anderson. Formally educated in Chemistry, Business, and Education, he is an educator, an author, a diverse entrepreneur, and he is the son of a disabled war veteran. "Walter the Educator" shares his time between educating and creating. He holds interests and owns several creative projects that entertain, enlighten, enhance, and educate, hoping to inspire and motivate you.

Follow, find new works, and stay up to date
with Walter the Educator™
at WaltertheEducator.com

www.ingramcontent.com/pod-product-compliance
Lightning Source LLC
LaVergne TN
LVHW010605070526
838199LV00063BA/5082